Rosemary for Remembrance

# Rosemary for Remembrance

Rosemary Anne Sisson

*The Radcliffe Press*
LONDON · NEW YORK

Published in 1995 by The Radcliffe Press
45 Bloomsbury Square, London WC1A 2HY
175 Fifth Avenue, New York NY 10010

A full CIP record for this book is available from
the British Library

A full CIP record for this book is available from
the Library of Congress

ISBN 1 86064 017 6

Library of Congress catalog card number: available

Printed and bound in Great Britain by
WBC Ltd, Bridgend, Mid Glamorgan

# Contents

# Illustrations

Those of us who were teenaged or in our twenties in 1939 look back and know that our whole lives were irreversibly changed by the War, that long, dark tunnel into which we trudged so reluctantly and from which we emerged five years later, half-triumphant, half-despairing, like actors in a play in which the first Act has been full of incident, but whose author has not yet decided what should happen in Acts Two and Three.

And then, when we looked about us, we found that some important characters were missing. We were not conscious of those great swathes of casualties suffered in the First War. Indeed, unless we were married to someone in the armed forces, we were almost too busy to notice those who died. It was as though this time, year by year, while we ourselves were struggling to survive, Death came and stealthily removed our friends. Even to someone like myself who was not married, there was a sensation of ghostly widowhood as I remembered those cousins and childhood friends with whom we went bathing and riding, played golf and tennis or with whom we went to our first grown-up dance, and found how many of them were dead or badly wounded, and all carried away from us like flotsam on the tide. So the War cast its shadow backwards upon that sunlit childhood as well as forward over an unknown and unforeseen future.

But the War wasn't all loss. There is some benefit in being so desperately miserable that you know you can never be *quite* so unhappy again. It is useful to be repeatedly so much afraid that you have charted for all time the height of your courage, the depth of your cowardice, the limit of your endurance. And it is good to know what it is to be really hungry, so that for the rest of your life you will remember that food, like education, is a privilege and that to waste it is a crime. Best of all, these were experiences which we all shared, which made us for a while one nation.

Just as the Old Contemptibles of the Great War have almost disappeared, so now we realise that *our* War, too, is fast slipping out of memory into history as that curious, bitter-sweet zest which has permeated all our lives vanishes with us into the grave. So, these poems are for those who died, those who lived to remember, and those who never knew.

*R.A.S.*

People-shaped people I see everywhere.
They walk in the streets and they breathe in the air.
Their eyes meet my eyes and their tongues speak to mine.
Their words are like water; their thoughts are like wine.

People-shaped people – how simple it seems
To turn their reality into my dreams.
But poets much wiser, more famous insist
That these people-shaped people I love don't exist.

A cruel disorder is art, they declare.
They make life a desert and dance in despair.
But to people-shaped people who, obstinate, live
These people-shaped poems I, obstinate, give.

# I  Country Matters

Did they really exist, those days when my sister and I
ran all summer barefooted in the fields, brought minnows and sticklebacks, newts and tadpoles back to the
home-made pond in the garden, when white fan-tailed
pigeons fed from our hands, when the countryside was
full of singing birds, and at night the barn-owl hooted
and the great cart-horses snorted and tore at the long
grass outside our bedroom windows?

My mother first saw John Bishop standing among
the bare, dripping branches in the garden at Lyminster.

'Come the spring,' he said, 'you'll think all the birds
of Sussex has got into the garden.' He pushed his old
cap back on his head. 'Regular charm of birds here,' he
said, 'in the spring.'

My parents never engaged Bishop. He simply told
them that he was the gardener and what his wages were.
I have a hundred pictures of Bishop in my mind. I see
his great, gnarled hands so delicately untangling a
hedgehog from the tennis netting, and see him shaking
his head in unsentimental regret over the little, furry
bodies of the nest of baby rabbits which he had dug out
in the orchard. I hear him say, 'There goes Jinny Wren!'
or 'There's Robbie!' and the birds who were his friends
became our friends, too. Their descendants sing in the
trees and bushes around Church Field to this day.

The time was to come when I would lie in that
narrow bed in that ground-floor bedroom under thatch,
listening to the thrrum-thrum! of German bombers
overhead, my little cardboard suitcase packed with my
novel, Edward Bear and the powder-blue suit and Juliet
cap bought for me by my mother at Swan and Edgar's
in those last foolish months of 1939 when we thought

that our lives were ours, all ours to spend. Still more alarming were the days in 1940 when there was an Army Sergeant on duty by the telephone and I lay and watched the lattice window above my head half expecting to see the shape of a German helmet telling me that the invasion had, indeed, begun.

Church Field is sold now, but my father is buried in the churchyard, next to the grave of Bishop and his wife who was also his childhood sweetheart, so we go back now and then to tend the graves. There are no more minnows or sticklebacks, tadpoles or newts. The streams are clogged or vanished and the water-cress beds and the Knucker Hole are fenced off and turned into a trout-farm, and the cart-horses were long ago replaced by tractors. We children, sleeping under thatch in unheated bedrooms, fetching milk in tin-cans from the farm and running barefoot in the fields were the last of the truly privileged. And yet I know that carefree country childhood, surrounded by love and beauty, armed and strengthened us for all that was to come.

# Privilege

Little girls in the grass, feeling with the fingers
Breast-feathers, pigeon-feathers, beaks in the palm
Tapping for wheat-seeds, timid yet demanding,
Breast-feathers, pigeon-feathers long, long ago.

Sunk sink in the grass, hands in the water
Cradling up orange-bellied, cream-bellied newts,
Tiny feet in the palm like damp, trusting twigs,
Prehistoric faces of long, long ago.

Cotton dresses hitched up in ice-cold water-meadows,
Feet on the smooth chalk feeling the flow
Of minnows and sticklebacks flicking round the instep,
Feet and fish in mud and water, long, long ago.

Vanished like the Trianon, that rustic aristocracy,
Claiming a privilege too great for humankind.
Little girls in cotton dresses, newts and sticklebacks
All gone together – oh, long, long ago!

# Love Song

When I am dead, I shall not have
A love for any single place,
My nation – possibly – angelic,
My domicile space.
But if I still can think of earth,
Though living in celestial light,
The fitful beauties of my Sussex
I will remember with delight.

When poised – my glowing wings unfurled
Upon a bright, ethereal ridge –
I shall recall the little stream
Beneath the unsteady wooden bridge,
The daisy-starred ten-acre field,
The primroses in Poling Wood,
And Chanctonbury Ring that high
Above the Downs in grandeur stood,
And how beneath the Church's tower
Stood close the old farm and the new,
And how on windy, stormy days,
The Knucker Hole shone midnight blue,

And how my heart belonged to Sussex.
All this, half-trembling, I'll recall –
And from my clear, celestial eye
A crystal tear – perchance – will fall.

# Michaelmas Daisy

A flower of classic innocence –
And yet not quite.
A slightly knowing purple tinge
Instead of white.

Straggling untidily about
The autumnal scene,
It emphasis less itself
Than what has been.

# Usually We Know Our Place

When sunset catches a sparrow's breast,
It turns as pink as a bird most rare.
So talent like genius briefly burns
In inspiration's flare.

# Blackbird, Lyminster

A blackbird singing in the rain
Is two parts joy and one part pain.
Of my whole life to come again,
I'd give it all for just that pain.


# Requiem for a Baby Blackbird, Parson's Green

To watch a blackbird die
It is a dreadful thing –
Never again to fly,
Never again to sing.

The parents in the lilac tree
Anguished they chink in vain.
The small brown feathers in the grass
Never will fly again,
And somewhere in instinctive heart
They feel a birdlike pain.

But, oh! this human heart
Attached to human brain,
Feels for those feathers in the grass
An all too human pain.

# The Blackbirds' Tragedy

There were two baby blackbirds,
Twins, as they seemed to be,
One knew what life was all about,
The other – oh dear me!

Simple and foolish bird,
It was devoid of fear.
It would let *me* come close to it.
What if a cat drew near?

We fed them, then they left.
I hoped it had survived,
But then, oh no! one summer's day
It blithely re-arrived.

Tail-less it was, but still
That perky look of pride.
It hopped about in ignorance of
Dangers on every side.

Its mother in attendance
Scuttled about in fear,
Using her warning cry to young –
This young one would not hear.

It hopped into the house,
And her pursuit was vain.
Fast as she drove it safely out,
It hopped back in again.

The father blackbird on the wall
It chinked. I knew its call.
It said, 'That foolish child
'It will destroy us all!'

Outside, beside the greenhouse,
I watched her, brave and true,
And, helpless, knew that if I moved
Disaster would ensue.

At last we two combined.
She led it out once more,
And sidling, breathless, I ran in
And safely closed the door.

But later from my study
That anxious 'cluck' I heard,
And knew the entrance down the steps
Had found that foolish bird.

Its tail-less tail triumphant,
It prinked about the floor.
The mother, following after, tried
To guide it out once more.

I tip-toed down. The mother
Flew hard against the glass.
Then she and I together
Contrived to let them pass

Safe out into the garden.
A flight of steps, no more,
I stopped to see them hip-hop up.
I wanted to be sure.

But this time it was different.
She had it on its back.
Her beak was striking at its throat
In desperate, mad attack.

I could not bear to watch
This chastening of her dear.
It would not heed her warning clucks.
She would try pain and fear.

I crept down late that evening
Before the darkness fell.
Just one black feather on the steps.
Thank heaven, all was well!

But no. Full light next morning
When I went down again
Revealed the truth – the baby bird
Dead in the outside drain.

Poor, cheerful little bird!
Dear God, she'd done her best!
But it had asked too much of her,
And now it was at rest.

But then – 'cluck, cluck' – I saw her
Come down the steps today,
Found that the little thing was gone,
And then she flew away,

But still throughout the morning
Clucked from the lilac tree,
The fact that she had killed her child
Lost from her memory.

Poor mangled little thing
Brought its own fate, and yet,
Bright as the blackbird sings its song,
I still can not forget.

# Fair's Fair

I never kill a caterpillar,
Since butterflies I love to see,
But how I wish he'd take his filla
Plants not *quite* so dear to me

(With apologies to Ogden Nash)

# Golden Wedding

Darling, wonderful Daphy-down-dilly,
Heart of my childhood, test of my life,
Always so brilliant, shrewd and discernible –
Feelings so tender, mind like a knife!

Dearly, oh dearly, I value that sisterhood.
Could I have lived without that other half?
Think of our dear Farmer Pring and his naming
Of Daphne and Rosemary, to each a calf!

Think of those bicycle rides up to Burpham,
Valley of Avillon claimed for our own,
Freedom and happiness, love, absurd innocence
Shared in that fellowship freely alone.

Then came at last on Arundel Station
A man, six-foot-three, who stepped down from the train
In a hat, *a pork pie?* Oh, good grief! But thank heaven!
Worn just to impress us, worn never again.

To Daphy and Patrick, so loving and generous,
I, fortunate spinster, acknowledge the debt
Quite unrepayable, children at one remove.
Thank you a thousand times always, and yet

Word can't repay the great gift that was granted.
I, Aunty Romy, your children may hold
Close to my heart, husbands, wives, children's children,
Shared immortality, dearer than gold.

# II   A Long War Ago

One of the worst things about a war is the way it banishes us all from the life we know. Even when your country isn't occupied by enemy troops, still it is occupied by war, and all the inhabitants are turned into refugees, dispossessed and forced to travel strange roads to nowhere.

At least the first months of the War were spent by us in Lyminster, so that extraordinary events acquired an absurdly comforting familiarity. We rushed out on to the tennis lawn to watch the dog-fights and, when a German plane was brought down, we bicycled off through those well-known lanes to find the wreckage. When a German pilot baled out and nearly landed in our garden but kicked his feet at the last minute, we were greatly disappointed that it was the Browns and not us who were offering him a cup of tea – especially when a dashing young Spitfire pilot arrived in an open two-seater, scarf thrown negligently round the neck of his uniform to visit his late opponent. And when Ford Aerodrome was bombed, my mother and father, my sister and I, and my Sealyham terrier, Beau, brown eyes astonished, ears flying in the wind of his indignant flight, dived, blind with terror, into dugouts which Bishop had dug in the front garden with the same methodical diligence with which he continued to dig trenches for Arun Banner potatoes in the back garden.

But clouds soon obscured the illusory sunshine. Exiled to Aberystwyth, working as a civilian secretary in the Royal Air Force, I knew that my life was over and that the war would never end. I sat in the hotel on the front which had been taken over as Headquarters of the Initial Training Wing, and I wrote poems as a shipwrecked sailor tries to quench his thirst with drops of rain.

My one ambition had always been to be an actress – oh, those incomparable performances as Juliet in the bathroom mirror! My parents, despite their evident dismay, promised me that if I took my School Certificate and gained Matriculation, I could go to a Drama School. I fulfilled my part of the bargain, but my parents were prevented from fulfilling theirs. Like many others of my generation, the War descended as an impenetrable barrier between me and my chosen career – all the more impenetrable because even to have personal hopes and ambitions in the midst of so much suffering and cruelty was not only impossible but even unthinkable.

Alarmed, I realised that when the War ended, if it ever did, I would be qualified for nothing but to be a shorthand-typist, and I worked as hard to get into the University as I had once worked to ensure my right to go to RADA. But in 1943, I knew that I could not go on studying Chaucer when my contemporaries were fighting and dying, and I volunteered for the WAAFS.

It was, of course, part of the general lunacy of War that, having braced myself for a brave dash into the unknown for the sake of my country, I was one of the first WAAFS to be seconded to the Royal Observer Corps. What's more, I was posted to Horsham in Sussex, so that I was able to live at home.

The University of London, with that arrogant wrongheadedness for which academics are rightly notorious, had decided that it was safe to bring University College back from Aberystwyth to Gower Street just in time for the second blitz and for my father's cherished and valuable library to be destroyed. He and my mother rented a bomb-damaged house in Chelsea, so, except for vacations, I was living alone, bicycling along the country road to Arundel Station, often late and night, and fre-quently through air-raids. But much worse than the fear of death was the fearful loneliness, and the discovery that our beloved Church Field, in solitary habitation, could become a house full of frightening creaks, whist-ling of wind and tapping of branches on windows. On the other hand, I must be one of the very few living creatures who has actually read from start to finish every single novel written by Walter Scott – and managed to write two unpublished novels in between.

Again, looking back, I realise that the Royal Observer Corps was perfectly designed for me. It was founded by civilian volunteers who like Dad's Army, came into their own when war was declared. On my first day's training, I sat between a bricklayer and a retired General. We plotted every aircraft which flew between Beachy Head and Selsey Bill and northwards to the borders of Surrey, and this included our own home aerodromes of Ford and Tangmere. It's odd to think that I probably plotted the sorties of Douglas Bader.

Odder still it is in these days when every Civil Servant seems to feel obliged to divulge secrets to Press or politicians to recall that we plotted some of the first of the Flying Bombs, having been informed of their existence some time before, and that, after coming on duty at midnight and finding the table entirely covered with plots of bombers, gliders and fighter planes, we returned home and, when our families exclaimed: 'The Invasion has begun!' we never replied, 'Yes. We know.' It was enough for us to know that we had plotted D-Day – the beginning of the end.

But it was not quite the end. One summer vacation – was it in 1944? – a Mosquito night-fighter pilot called Russell Stewart used to come and have tea with us. He told us hilarious stories of narrow escapes and absurd misunderstandings, but we knew in our hearts that when we left him alone in a deck-chair on the lawn surrounded by honeysuckle and roses that he was escaping from the unacknowledged terror of that most treacherous of planes and most perilous of assignments. Then he stopped coming. I often wondered if he survived.

One grey winter's day in 1945, I'd slept until teatime, having been on duty all night. I was just making myself a piece of toast when I heard the plane flying low, then lower. There were tall elm trees bordering the farm-yard. You can still see where one is missing.

The war did end at last and we all danced in the streets, but we were all so tired and cold and hungry that it seemed as though it had been a kind of sickness from which we would never quite recover. I took a B.A. at University College, London and an M. Lit. at Cambridge, but I still felt defeated. Then, in 1949, I was invited to go and teach in the University of Wisconsin in America and I went, like a rat leaving a sinking ship.

I only stayed in Wisconsin for a year, but that was enough to set me free. The great gift which the United States gives – or then gave – was the belief that anything is possible, and that human beings must aspire to the best, and know that they can achieve it if they try hard enough, but that it is up to them, landing penniless and alone on some strange and distant shore, to decide whether or not they care to fight for their destiny.

Ten years after the war ended, safe, happy, and with my feet set upon the path which, I suppose, they were always meant to travel, I went back to Aberystwyth, that little Welsh seaside town where, at seventeen years old, I had been so sure that the war would never end, and that my life was over.

# A Long War Ago

Was this how it happened to me
A long war ago?
Did I hear the elm-tree go,
See golden tracer-bullets fly,
And fear to come too close,
And in the lane stand watching two men die?

Was terror just like that
When flying bombs cut out?
A silent, anguished shout
Of hope that it would fall elsewhere,
And in that hope fulfilled
Came those sick bedfellows, relief and shamed despair?

Does there exist somewhere
That trembling other me,
Resistless refugee,
Driven from all that it could trust and know,
Caught in a trap of pity for itself
And all who suffered that long war ago?

# Epitaph, 1940

He would soon have retired (he was getting stout).
He'd have mowed the lawn a bit, and pottered about
The house, 'doing odd jobs,' he called it, whereas she
Would have done the shopping, some housework, had
    Mary to tea
('My eldest girl, her husband's a gunner, you know'),
And also young Robert ('who does love doughnuts so').
While Jane, their youngest, training up at Guys,
Was engaged to a nice young man who, selling ties,
Was swept away in a very short time to train
For the Navy. Now he's at sea. ('It's hard on Jane.')

Doing harm to no one, being harmed by none,
They hoped to live till their quiet time was done.
They asked one thing, and when that was denied,
Together, in their suburban house, they died.

# Aircraft Recognition

'That,' I said, looking with interest
Up at the sky,
'Is a Blenheim bomber,
'(British)' I added, in parenthesis.
Fortunately, although the blast of the bombs
Knocked me down, I was quite unhurt.

'I always think,' I remarked casually,
'That Spitfires are so graceful in the air.
'Look at that one, for example,
I added, 'I like to see them about;
'They make one feel
'So safe.'
The machine-gun bullets missed me, I'm glad to say,
Though a tile from the roof hit me on the head.

'Look,' I shouted in wild excitement,
'That's a Messerschmitt. Get under cover!'
I dived under a hedge
And lay very still.
''Ere, Dorrie,' said the small evacuee from next door,
'See that 'Urricane?'

# Family Pride and the Morrison Shelter

How sad to think that my Aunt Mabel
Was killed while underneath a table!

One feels that one could write a saga
On someone killed while drinking lager.

Or, if the bomb fell as she dined –
But Aunt beneath *her* board reclined.

How sad to think that my Aunt Mabel
Died while underneath a table!

# Aberystwyth, 1942

Have you seen the porpoises rolling in the bay?
Have you seen the black rocks dancing in the spray?
Have you seen the shadows on the distant mountains,
　　　Blue and purple and grey?
Have you seen the heaving of the grey-bosomed sea?
Have you seen the green buds on every hedge and tree?
Have you seen the birds waking up to the Spring
　　　And singing joyfully?

Where blue-grey smoke rose to join the clouds
From the small, neat houses of the London crowds,
Charred spirals leave the blackened stones
　　　Which are their shrouds.
Blinded by the thought of all that pain,
How can we see the sun and the rain
And the hills and the sea and the lambs? Dear God,
　　　Give us back Spring again!

# Beacon, 30/5/42

'In the deep and careful blackness of our German night,
'Leaps a high and glorious beacon swiftly into sight.'

'Is it lit to shine the thankful wanderers to their rest?
'Does it call the silver birds pulsing to their nest?'

'Hark, I hear them beating high above the flood-lit earth,
'Turning now to cups of coffee, anecdotes and mirth.'

'Is the glow not rather great, burns it not afar
'Even to the silent twinkle of the furthest star?'

'Ah, but there are many of them; still I hear them fly,
'Throbbing, throbbing, never-ending in the tender sky.'

'Are there not some other beacons? Is there just the one?
'Will each silver bird arrive at that one midnight sun?'

'Ah, it is a noble beacon, glowing there alone,
'While the engines beat above it.' 'Hush! It is Cologne!'

# Canteen Dance, Initial Training Wing, Aberystwyth

The room was warm with many dancers,
With many-coloured dresses bright,
Grey-blue tunics and whitened belts
Under the tinsel-bedecked light.

One flight to go on leave next Monday.
Laughter and clapping, noisy cheers,
Mock-anger from the disappointed.
This was no time for tears.

A group of young fools formed a circle,
Joined hands and sang and stamped their feet,
Their eyes alight with pleased excitement,
Their faces shining with the heat.

Seeing them so foolish and light-hearted,
Debt unincurred still to be paid,
Was I alone suddenly clutched with pity?
Was I alone cold and afraid?

# Fighter Pilot's Wife

Because, whatever we may say or do,
You and I
Will always have that vision clear of you
In the sky.

Because you, who are young and strong of limb,
Will have no power
To avert your destiny, so bright and grim,
In that hour.

Because, through all our warm and casual mirth,
You and I
Can always see you flaming down to earth
Across the sky.

# Commonplace, 1943

Their engines beating an even rhythm
(Men look up from their work at the sound),
Wing-tip to wing-tip they fly in formation –
Thirty-six Spitfires outward bound.

Slim and yet sturdy, like well-bred terriers,
Each independent yet part of the whole,
Fierce but dispassionate, steady yet eager,
Thirty-six Spits on offensive patrol.

Over the coast-line see them returning,
Skimming like wild-fowl close to the ground.
Men glance upwards to watch them flying –
Thirty-five Spitfires homeward bound.

# Epitaph on an Airman

Sweet earth, rest gently on my friend.
Although he did not love you half as well as the wide sky.
Yet here must lie
At this his brief life's end.

Sweet flowers, grow freshly on his grave.
Although my friend had little time in which to hold you
    dear,
Yet blossom here,
And make this drab earth brave.

Sweet Lord, take to thy keeping this my friend.
Although his heart and courage were forever high,
Fear lurked close by.
Let him find Thee and safety at his last flight's end.

# Routine Flight, Mosquito, 1945

Beastly chilly afternoon,
White and still,
O.K. be back soon.
Come on, Bill.
    Blasted boots,
    Parachutes.
    O.K., Flight,
    She's all right.

Good take-off from the 'drome,
With luck, you'll see,
We'll be home
In time for tea.
    Nice warm Mess,
    Wireless,
    Toast and jam,
    And – oh, damn!
    Forgot to write
    That card to Bet.
    Have to get
    It off tonight.

Now we're back.
Bill, can you – ?
Yes, there's Jack
Airborne, too.
    Here we go
    Swooping low,
    With Jack
    Some way back.
    Under us pass
    Downland grass,

Trees in clumps,
Houses in lumps,
Like a kid's toy bricks,
Roads, bridges, streams,
Like you see 'em in dreams,
The whole bag of tricks.

Bloody fine plane to fly,
Makes you feel
You're riding high,
Half unreal,
But solid too,
Safe and strong –
Hey, Jack, how long
Do we wait for you?

Here we go.
At-a-girl!
Flying low –
'Makes their hair curl.
Makes you feel good,
Climbing up steeply,
Diving down deeply,
Skimming a wood.
A splutter, a cough,
Both engines off.
Still in a dive.
Down to zero-five.
Diving still.
Makes you lose your breath.
My God! Sorry, Bill.
This is it.   This is death.

# Goodbye to London, 1949

It is goodbye to London, then,
Her tumbled walls and hollow towers,
Her vacant sites, like missing teeth,
Incongruous with small wild flowers.

It is goodbye to London, then,
The broken houses by the Thames,
The masonry, the dust, the dirt,
All that is left by blast and flames.

It is goodbye to weary queues,
Goodbye, full buses in the rain,
Goodbye, tired people, empty hands,
But oh my city in the rain,
I will, I will be back again.

# Return to Aberystwyth

But to return, but to return after so long –
Not to the ignorant green fields of childhood,
But to the bitter pavements of my youth,
Where on these slipping, alien, slate-chip hills,
An all-unmothered Ruth,
New-widowed of long husbanded innocence,
Finding unhappiness a kind of sin,
I walked and cried those tears which, cried but once,
Make such a breach irreconcilable
Between the self and life, as death itself
Cannot quite serve to mend it.
Here I died.
Here is this small Welsh town I see my dying,
Here, with the graves of seamen, is my lying.
Oh, young, lost seafarer, drowned in despair,
And never guessed that from the white bones tossing
The coral hope would blossom, sad seas under.
But to return, but to return after so long!

# III First Rehearsal

It seems strange to me now, looking back, to realise how long it took me to discover that the true fulfilment of my life did not lie in being an actress, but in writing parts which actors and actresses would love to play and plays which audiences would love to watch. When at last it happened, I was like Florence Nightingale when she was finally allowed to train as a nurse – even if it was only scrubbing floors. It was as though my life had been a jig-saw which wouldn't fit and suddenly God put the missing piece into my hand and it all came together – not into the picture I was trying to make, but quite a different and much more satisfying one.

It was all the stranger because my father was a Shakespearean scholar and editor, so that we always knew that the plays were written by a craftsman as well as a genius. Like children brought up in an artist's studio, we were aware of the tools of Shakespeare's trade and of the cunning with which he used them. When my father retired from his professorship, he was offered the post of first Senior Fellow at the Shakespeare Institute in Stratford-upon-Avon. My parents bought a cottage in Tyler Street, which used to be called Donkey Row and was a few hundred yards from the house where William was born. To all of us, living in Stratford was like moving into the house of a beloved friend.

In 1951, there was a famous production of the History Plays at what was then called the Memorial Theatre in Stratford. Following the story from Richard the Second to Henry the Fifth was, I must now confess, like watching *Coronation Street* or *Upstairs, Downstairs* and seeing the characters develop as their fortunes changed, especially since Harry of Monmouth was played by that marvellous unknown young Welsh actor with the magnetism of Olivier but with his own haunting quality of voice and personality, Richard Burton. So I came home and looked it up in Holinshed's Histories, and found that, after Henry the Fifth died, his young widow, Katherine de Valois, fell in love with a handsome Welsh soldier called Owen Tudor, and from their union derived the Tudor dynasty. Shakespeare must have read this, too, since this was the book he used for his research, but, the marriage between Owen and Katherine being more than a little dodgy, he must have decided to skip that one. So I wrote the play which Shakespeare didn't write, and I called it *The Queen and the Welshman*. In 1957, when I had completely rewritten it seven times and also written seven more plays as well, it was produced on the fringe of the Edinburgh Festival. It never reached the West End, but when two of the other plays were produced on consecutive years, I knew that I was on my way and that my life's joy and my life's work had come together.

# Stratford Sonnet

Not like some peevish fugitive from death,
Disputing life's completeness with the tomb,
Nor, grossly garmented in all but breath,
Treading the boards of some frequented room –

No, spirits do not show skull-dwindled faces,
Nor lift their melted eyelids out of sleep,
But gentleness still keeps familiar places,
And country memories are long and deep.

The swans, strong-beating in the evening air,
Call you, with us, to note their tuneful pride,
And doubled pleasure is it still to share
The kingcups, prodigal on Water-side.

Waking, with you we lie and listen still
To cuckoos calling, up on Welcombe Hill.

# Shakespeare at Coventry

Time, like a flood, high monument entombs,
Engulfs whole cities in its silent waste,
Dwindles great empires into little rooms,
Turns pomp to history, glory to 'taste'.

Art and religion stand against the flood,
Breaking the waters of oblivion,
Yet even they stand rooted in the mud,
Targets for ignorance and derision.

How then can Shakespeare still his vantage hold,
Unchallenged sculptor of humanity?
But that his truth and love like purest gold
Endure unchanged the all-corroding sea.

So Coventry's Church time's fury shall abate,
Love rising, Phoenix-like, from war and hate.

# Prologue to *As You Like It*
## Played before Queen Elizabeth II
## at Stratford, 1957

When Rosalind first won Orlando's heart,
And banished Duke did his first state maintain,
The Globe sufficed to hold that poet's art
Which the wide world can scarcely now contain.

Five hundred years has shone this Stratford star,
Yet fifty-two of life his mortal span,
As in one Crown Empires prefigured are,
Undying plays immortalise this man.

To please a Queen our Shakespeare then did write
(Yet half expectant of this later day)
When from an English heart he did indite
What we now in the heart of England play.

To please a Queen are our endeavours spent.
Ma'am, if you like it, we are well content.

# In Celebration of £100 Prize Offered for a New Play in Memory of William Shakespeare

*Actor*  And, for star-billing? Surely, William Shakespeare!

*Manager*  He *must* appear! So many thoughts upon him!

Why – immortality, it's just a word.

To say you are remembered. 'William Shakespeare'.

Why, we created him. We gave him life.

If we'd not read his plays, not acted them,

His very tombstone, worn as smooth as glass,

Would give reflection of a thousand feet.

Treading upon his unremembered dust.

And of himself no image give at all.

    *Actor*  He must appear. He owes it to his creators.

    *Poet*  A new play, then, and call it – *William Shakespeare?*

    *Manager*  Yes, certainly. Leave the main part – a blank.

    *Actress*  A blank, my Lord. She never told her love.

    *Manager*  Enough! We will have no Shakespearean

echoes.

    *Actor*  But we are speaking in Shakespearean verse.

    *Manager*  Then let us cease to do so.

    (Pause)

    *Poet*                                          Long caesura!

Dramatic verse. It tumbled into the grave

When Shakespeare died. One heavy-footed mourner

Drank semi-prosaic cocktails on the tomb.

Another, more light-footed, danced a little,

His Venus burned, his Boy the darkness lit,

But that fair flood, that spring of poetry

Which made the English stage the dream of Kings

Sank into Stratford's earth whence it had sprung.

And never, never will come forth again.

*Manager*  Find some new poetry.

*Poet*                                    There is none so apt.
To speak and sing, be angry, love and laugh,
And all in idiom of the English tongue.

*Manager  There is a hundred pounds reward!*

*Poet*                                    I know.

(Pause)

*Actor*  Write in the Auden style. Come, be obscure.
Men must admire what they don't understand.

*Poet*  I'm trying to do so, but that limpid mind.
That crystal-clear yet convoluted style
Keeps driving me towards this damned blank verse.

*Manager*  Oh, for God's sake, let's speak in prose!

*Actress*                                    Awhile.

*Manager*  I beg your pardon?

*Actress*                      'Speak in prose awhile.'
        (apologetically)
It made the rhythm better.

*Manager*              Damn the rhythm!
Will no one rid us of this William Shakespeare?

*Poet*  So now we have the truth of it at last.
We come to bury Shakespeare, not to praise him.
And if he wrote now *Hamlet, Lear, Othello*.
There is no theatre in the British Isles
Would put those plays on for a hundred pounds.

# First Rehearsal, 'The Queen and the Welshman'

Dust in their silent mouths,
Housed in cold lead,
Each in a grave alone
The lovers lay dead.

His sixty-year-old bones
Brittle and lean,
She childbed-died and laid
Rich like a Queen.

Far miles between them stood.
Echoing years
Dried from each hollow skull
Warm blood and tears.

Could some weak summoning
Bring them again
Flesh to the dwindled bone,
To the heart, pain,

Would she, Eurydice,
Back from the dead,
Claim with her Welsh Orpheus
That love-tossed marriage bed?

Or, keeping death's surcease,
Would each remain
Close in the narrow grave,
Summoned in vain?

Chairs in a circle stood.
Lines rang like charms.
And the lovers of Hatfield came
To each other's arms!

# The Vagrant Heart

As I went out on the road
On a morning in May,
I saw a girl with black hair
Going my way.
I said to her, 'Where you go,
I will be there.'
She said, 'Go where you will.
I do not care.'

So she before me went,
Raining or shine,
Till at noon in the shade
We stopped to dine.
I said to her, 'Sit by me.
'My food I'll share.'
She said, 'I'll sit where I please.
'I've my own fare.'

So she went on before,
While the sun shone,
Till towards eventide,
When night drew on,
I said to her, 'Sleep with me,
Here in my arm.'
She said, 'I'll build me a fire
'To keep me warm.'

So I lay all night long
And could not sleep,
Till towards morningtime, she 'gan to weep.
'My fire is gone out,' she says, 'and I am chill.'

'Come,' says I, 'sleep with me.'
Says she, 'I will.'

Then we together went,
Both she and I,
Until one day in the wintertime
Did my girl die.
And now when I go on the road,
Both night and day,
I see a girl with black hair
Going my way.

# The Royal Captivity

Come, my lass, come away wi' me,
Come, my ain, tae the Northland.
I will gi' thee a silver ring,
If thou wilt be my ain one.
I will gi' thee a pair o' shoon,
And an eagle's feather.
We will find the road to Scotland,
And we'll dwell there taegither,
We'll dwell there taegither.

Blue the hills in the twilight glow,
Faint the track through the heather,
Few the folk who will wish us well,
Wintry and drear the weather.
Still the note of the curlew's cry
Bids us journey onwards.
Though the road be rough to Scotland,
We'll be travelling hamewards,
We'll be travelling hamewards.

Come, my lass, gi' me now thy hand.
Here is mine for a token.
May the vows that we make this day
Never be spent or broken.
Soon we'll be i'the land I lo've,
Nevermore to leave her.
We will take the road to Scotland,
And we'll dwell there forever,
And we'll dwell there forever.

# M.C.

Heart's dearest love, though dead so long,
And dead or ever I was born,
This high-flown phrase befits a love
So foolish, high-flown and forlorn.

The intellect which charms me most,
The warmth and generosity,
Still glows with life, so easily
Outliving half a century.

But cold the flesh, and alien still
The land, the tongue, the hurling-field,
The pubs, the swearing, and the dream;
Yet to the man I still must yield.

The man, so laughing, tender, true,
Ferocious, loyal, generous, brave,
Commands at last, though useless now,
The love till now I never gave.

So across time and space
My heart to yours must wing,
As now my body goes
To Ireland in the Spring.

# Liberation

It was my thirtieth year to heaven
Like a friendly midwife came,
Ended the long pregnancy,
And freed the infant from the womb.

Not through any miracle
Came this child upon the earth,
Yet he was of virgin born,
And heaven smiled upon his birth.

In the instant lost and gained,
Close handfasted and yet free,
In my thirtieth year to heaven
Came my spirit home to me!

# IV  Sing a Song of Galilee

One of my favourite writers is Henry Thoreau, the American philosopher who went to prison for refusing to pay taxes because he didn't approve of the way the Government spent his money. (Most of us, I imagine, have an affinity with him in that respect.) But I love him above all for the way in which he died. When he was on his death-bed, some New England busybody asked him if he had made his peace with God. Henry Thoreau replied, 'We have never quarrelled.'

I do understand the urgent missionary feeling of evangelists, and, as a Christian, I truly long to share my blessing with others. But somehow I cannot take to people who come up to me and say 'Have you found Jesus?' I feel like replying, 'I have never lost him.'

From my earliest days, Jesus, like Shakespeare, has been an essential part of my life. We went to Church, as we went to the theatre and the cinema, together, as a family, and it was natural for me to act out the New Testament story in my mind, to imagine what it would be like to be one of the Disciples, to know the wonder and excitement of recognising the Messiah, the horror of the betrayal and the crucifixion, the incredulous joy of the Resurrection and, after Jesus was received up to heaven, to know what it was to be the first Christians who had to face the hard grind of making Christianity – that most testing of all religions – work down there in that tough, workaday world.

So it was nothing strange to me to find Christ as much a part of the wartime experiences as he had been part of my childhood and early youth, and when the bombers came, I used to lie in bed and take hold of the sheet and pretend that I was taking hold of the robe of

Jesus, there in the crowd, and saying, 'Help me, Lord,' I knew, of course, that it wasn't really a fold of Jesus' garment, but just the thin cotton turned sides-to-middle sheet on the narrow bed in which I had slept since I was six years old, but it helped all the same.

In 1952, I went on a pilgrimage to the Holy Land which was organised by the Vicar of our church in Chelsea. The city of Jerusalem was still divided and the war of 1948 was fresh and heroic in the minds of the Israelis. The waiter who served us coffee had on his arm the number of the concentration camp in which he had been imprisoned. But our Israeli guide, Miron, compared the recent battle to the battles of Joshua, and as we drove up the straight road to Jerusalem, we sang the song he taught us: '*Evenu shalom aleichem.*' '*Shalom Aleichem*' – 'Peace be unto you' – the words which Christ said when he came back to his friends in that upper room in Jerusalem after his death.

Some people are disappointed when they go to the Holy Land, but to me it all became suddenly rooted in reality. Instead of those golden-haired virgins and fat pink babies pictured by Renaissance painters, I saw the dark-eyed girl who welcomed us into her house in the little town of Cana in Galilee – where Jesus turned the water into wine. Nazareth had a steep, narrow street where a carpenter might live and work. The Garden of Gethsemane was still there on the hill outside Jerusalem, and we walked down the rocky path where Christ rode on Palm Sunday. And, despite the intrusive churches with their garish lights and dubious claims and absurd relics, we were able to see an upper room exactly like the one where Jesus ate the Last Supper, and Gordon's Tomb showed us how the stone was rolled away from the entrance and allowed us to sit in a quiet garden and imagine that moment when the man Mary thought to be the gardener called her by her name and she said: 'Rabboni!'

There is a Lido now on the Lake of Galilee where once we saw fisherman pulling in their nets. The Negev Desert blossoms like a rose – or rather, with avocados – and high rise flats have been built outside Nazareth. The needs of a modern urban state have devoured the Holy Land we knew. Worse still, the gentle, dignified Israelis who were our hosts and who were so proud to have at last their own land again have had to turn into fierce and ruthless fighters in order to retain it.

And then, again, the country I left to visit the Holy Land in 1952 was a Christian country, whereas now we know what it is to have a Bishop of Durham who does not believe in the Resurrection and to find it hard to remember when we last heard the Archbishop of Canterbury quote the words of Jesus to us, speaking heart to heart as on the road to Emmaus. But then Christianity was never meant to be a dogma of mass belief like communism. Each of us must find our own way to the foot of the Cross, and beyond.

# Good Friday

I saw him in the radiance of a bright spring morning.
I looked at him and smiled at him and went my way,
For I knew him and I liked him, but he was not my true
    love,
The one who would hold me forever and a day.

I saw him in the bloom of a warm summer's evening,
With scent of roses and a thrush's song.
I nodded my acquaintance and turned to wander,
For surely I should find my love before very long.

I saw him in the autumn with the Michaelmas daisies,
When chrysanthemums were blowing and my hands were
    cold.
I frowned at him and stamped my foot and turned my
    shoulder,
For he was not my true love and I was growing old.

The skies were grey and shadowed and the earth was
    darkened.
I heard from the hill-top a cry of despair.
And I wept then and trembled and knew him for my true
    love,
And crept to the gallows' foot to see him there.

# Fred + Hoyle = ?

'Mathematics is God,' said Fred.
God smiled and did a calculation
How many gods small men had made
Since he completed their creation.

# Easter, 1946

Blackthorn in bloom, and the cuckoo is singing,
The sky it is blue and the wind it blows cold.
There's light in my heart and the church bells are ringing.
Daisies are white, and the dandelions gold.

'Christ, Christ, Jesus is risen!'
These are the words you can hear the birds say.
'Christ, Christ, Jesus is risen!'
Easter is here. Christ is risen today.

# New Year, 1948

Ring in the new, ring out the old
Courage and visions, now grown cold.

Ring out the old, ring in the new,
New wars, new fears and hopes too few.

Ring out old loyalties and kindness.
Ring in new prejudice and blindness.

Ring out the faith in God I owed –
Ring in that faith once more bestowed!

In all the sorrow and the pain,
Let that one constant still remain.

# New Year's Eve, 1955

So the year,
Like a dancer, like a guest,
Silently comes to rest,
Menacingly takes leave,
Now, on this darkening eve,
And leaves me here.

He came first to my door
New-born, unknown,
But now, a tyrant lover, a son full-grown,
There on the stage sinks with my pleasure,
There at the threshold departs with my treasure,
And leaves me poor.

But, hark! through the pain,
That flawless, new-born cry
Which no man can deny.
Laid in the self-same manger
As that other stranger –
Welcome, New Year, welcome again!

# New Year's Eve, 1960

Babe new-born, babe new-born, what do you hope for?
Warm milk, warm arms, nothing to fear.
Man dying, man dying, what do you hope for?
A bier.

Ah, babe, poor babe, hope without warrant,
Self-intent singleness, nothing to share!
Ah man, ah man, Croesus would envy –
Golden with pity, rich with despair!

ABOVE. Lyminster Church and Farm.
BELOW. Rosemary and Daphne feeding pigeons at Lyminster.

Patrick and Daphne Lister, 1st October, 1942
(Rosemary as bridesmaid on the right).

ABOVE. Woman Observer R. A. Sisson, 1943.
BELOW. Captain C. J. Sisson, Home Guard, Bishop, the Gardener,
my mother, Beau, Rosemary, Lyminster, 1943.

ABOVE. Edward Woodward as Owen Tudor, Edward Burnham as the Duke of Gloucester and Hilary Liddell as Katherine de Valois in *The Queen and the Welshman,* 1957.

BELOW. *Upstairs, Downstairs,* "A Patriotic Offering", with, clockwise, Jenny Tomasin, Christopher Beeny, Jean Marsh, Gordon Jackson, Angela Baddeley, Jacqueline Tong.

Rosemary with 'Flash', the pit-pony hero of Walt Disney's
*Escape from the Dark*.

ABOVE. Rosemary with the Director, Charles Jarrett, looking at a re-write on location for *Escape from the Dark*.
BELOW. Jodie Foster, David Niven and Helen Hayes in my third Walt Disney film, *Candleshoe*.

ABOVE. Rosemary with David Niven on location for *Candleshoe,*
laughing at the accidental *double entendre* he has just
written in autographing his book for her.
BELOW. Rosemary with Walt Disney animators working on
*The Black Cauldron.*

ABOVE. The Morley Family – left to right, Annabel, Sheridan, Robert, Joan, Wilton.
BELOW. Rosemary with Pierce Brosnan at the party in Parson's Green after the filming of the T.V. mini-series, *The Manions of America*.

ABOVE. *The Irish R. M.* team on location – left to right, Rosemary, Beryl Reid, Faith Brook, Brendan Conroy, Lise-Ann McLaughlin, Doran Godwin, Anna Manahan, Bryan Murray, Peter Bowles.

LEFT. My father in the last happy years as Senior Fellow at the Shakespeare Institute, Stratford-upon-Avon.

ABOVE. Reunion at Newnham College – left to right, Jill, née Woolner, Rosemary, Muriel, née Clarke (Jeanette, née Green, taking the photograph).
BELOW. My mother in the garden in Parson's Green with her 80th Birthday present, a portable telephone.

ABOVE. Celebrating the new Bell Chamber in Lyminster Church
given in memory of my father – left to right, The Duchess of Norfolk,
Rosemary, my mother, Daphne, Janet Hopkins,
Head Bellringer. (Photograph by Aperture).

BELOW. *The Young Indiana Jones* team at Skywalker Ranch – left to right,
Frank Darabont, Anne Merrifield, Rosemary, Gavin Scott, George Lucas,
Jonathan Hensleigh, Jule Selbo, Matthew Jacobs, Debby Fine,
Jane Bay, Jonathan Hales.

My first episode for *The Young Indiana Jones Chronicles*, "London, 1916" – from left to right,
Frederick Treves, Sean Patrick Flannery, Elizabeth Hurley, Vanessa Redgrave
(By kind permission of George Lucas).

# Twelfth Man

Joyful the bells of Easter, and the sound
Leaping and tumbling in the golden air,
Tulips and scent of lilac, and the birds
Singing, and flowers blooming on the graves.
Only his face was dark amidst the light.

'Sunshine,' he said, 'and just so blue a sky
'The day we came down to Jerusalem.
'We said that it was madness. So it was,
'And would have led to trouble even if –
'For then another would have. Why should he
'Endanger others and betray himself?
'I told him it was madness, and he smiled
'As though he reasoned with a spoilt son,
'And scolded me for what he called my fears –
'Well, teased me, then, for he would rarely scold,
'But reasoned gravely when he most was moved,
'And smiled at us when others would have frowned,
'Until we saw by gazing in our hearts
'The evil or the folly we had thought –
'Well, so the others said, but as for me,
'Always it seemed that I was in the right,
'And he, who erred, still put me in the wrong,
'Not in his own eyes only, but mine, too.

'And yet, when I had left him, stood alone,
'Pondered on all his words, I realised
'That he, the Promised One, was weak and soft,
'Fearful and unambitious, yet no less
'Reckless when there was nothing in the world
'To gain from courage. I recall the day

'Inside the Temple when a simple scribe
'Asked him if tribute should be paid to Rome.
'Then was the time – so clear to all but him! –
'For a distinct avowal of his strength.
'Then the Messiah, sent indeed by God,
'Would have arisen in his noble wrath,
'Called on the people, ended tyranny,
'Then, when his spell was fresh, our love was strong.
'But, while the scribe waited for his reply,
'And while the people waited eagerly,
'He gazed upon the man until he shrank,
'And looked at us as though he knew our thoughts,
'And answered with a Pharisean quibble,
'And once again it seemed that we were wrong.

'There is a memory I cannot lose –
'An upper room, a table long and bare,
'And fellowship most honest, warm and kind,
'And one best-loved who leant upon his breast.
'I was a member of that fellowship.
'I – I did sit and eat the Passover.
'Yes, I was one of them, of that small band,
'And they, my comrades, trusted me to death.
'But when I ate the bread and turned to him,
'He looked at me, into my silent heart,
'And in his look was pity, pain, regret,
'But was no trust. He trusted all but me.
'And all, all trusted me, save he alone.

'What could I do but go, being no more his,
'To find the High Priest and the men of Law?
'What could I lose, since I had lost his trust,
'Though not his love. I could not lose his love.
'If I had been a sinner like the girl

'Who washed her sins by washing of his feet,
'Why then there might have been a hope for me.
'But I was still a strong and upright man,
'Read in the Law and knew all God's commands.
'How could I crawl to him as though I sinned?
'And so I left, went slowly down the steps,
'And through the silent, still, familiar streets,
'And went to those who had contempt for me,
'But did not love me. Pride repels contempt.

'There was no need for weapons or for staves.
'I could have told them – knew we'd find him there
'Unarmed and unprepared for violence –
'The mighty warrior who should free our Race!
'I stepped up to him in Gethsemane
'And took his hand and kissed him on the cheek,
'And greeted him with "Master", our old name,
'For so I thought I might for this last time.
'He turned his head and smiled and called me "Friend".
'Oh, God! How could he call me by that name,
'And smile that way, and speak to me so low,
'As though we two had met at last alone,
'As though the world stood back to watch us meet!

'No man could bear the weight of so much love,
'Or live for countless years in ignorance
'If he'd betrayed the Chosen One of God,
'Or helped the downfall of a crazy fool.
'I took the silver, sticky with his blood,
'And slimy with their breath who gave it me.
'I tried to buy him back, that he once more
'Might reason with me, win my love again,
'Tell me I erred or mourn my little faith,
'For I had followed him too long, too long,

'To free myself now swiftly from his spell.
'They laughed at me, and one said, "crucified",
'And then I knew at last what I had done,
'And flung the money down, and fled alone
'Into the darkness and the winds of death.'

The birds sang sweetly. I was there alone
With scent of lilac and the Easter hymn.

# Galilee

Among the green hills and the valleys of Galilee
I heard a voice that I knew long ago.
I smelled the sweet scent of the wild flowers of Galilee,
Treading the paths where his feet used to go.

There is peace in the streets of the small towns of Galilee,
Barley and wheat in the fields turning gold.
Young men push their boats out on the blue sea of Galilee,
Haunting the mind with the fishers of old.

I am far away now from the green hills of Galilee.
Never in life shall I see them again.
But wherever I go, I'll be walking in Galilee.
Safe in my heart it will ever remain.

# Low Churchmen

Jesus, so gentle with men's little foibles,
Turning the water into wine,
Jesus, so easy with Sabbath-breaking,
Plucking the wheat in the bright sunshine,
Would he have scolded his simple children
Who climb to his heart by a cross of gold,
Or would he have held his arms wide open,
Said, 'Suffer them still!' as in days of old?

# The Mountain

We climbed in fellowship
And hardly felt the climb.
We walked about and smiled
And spent the wasteful time.

We talked about the view.
We felt no urgency,
As though a timelessness
Must tend such ecstasy.

The summit and the clouds
Became an instant one.
We shared a rapture there,
And found ourselves alone.

And then we turned our eyes
Towards the sleeping town,
And – 'Oh, Lord!' said Peter,
'It's a long way down!'

# The True Miracle

'How was it? Was it like this? Silver stars on a blue robe,
    flowers in your hair?'
'No, it was mud floor, and a mud-bricked house, and flies,
    flies everywhere.'
'How was he when he came? Noble and fair, a lily in his
    hand?
'And did you there in the garden demurely before him
    stand?'
'No, it was rending pain and fear, and when he was gone,
    the retching still,
'And only breath enough to whisper, "Ah God – thy
    Will!"'
'But there was a difference, wasn't there, later on, after
    the Child was born and laid in the straw,
'And everyone knew you were a lady forever more?'
'I stooped like the other women for thorns for the fire,
    and made my bread,
'And narrowly lived in dirt and disease, and feared to be
    dead.'
'But afterwards, there at Jerusalem, there by the Cross,
    proudly you knew who had died?'
'I felt more grief than other women, but no more pride.'
'But now you knew yourself for all eternity the interceder
    one for another.'
'No, I remembered the bitter, true day He said, "I have
    no mother."'
'But you were the Queen of Heaven who all her golden
    life walked where the angels have trod.'
'No! A poor woman of Israel, and yet to me, O miracle!
    was born our God!'

# Carol for Today

Jesus Christ was born today –
God forgive us all!
He who all the world would sway,
They laid him in a stall.

Cold the straw which made his bed,
Cold was Mary's cheer.
Still she nestled close his head,
Comforted her dear.

All the world about them went,
Never glanced their way,
Never guessed that he was sent
To save us all today.

Till the shepherds on the hill,
Silent in the night,
Heard voices in the frosty still,
Saw the angel light.

Till the wise men from afar
Dreamt a wondrous thing,
Following a brilliant star,
Hailed him as their King.

Then the people, crowding near,
Sang a joyous hymn,
Promised for a thousand year
They'd remember him.

Another woman came next day –
God forgive us all! –

Found that she her child must lay
Naked in the stall.

Jesus Christ was born today.
Now then let us bring
Hearts as fresh as Christians may,
Presents for our King.

## Christmas in Parson's Green

In Parson's Green in Fulham
They put the lighted tree
By the uncurtained window
For passers-by to see.

A welcome in the kitchen,
A pot-plant in the hall,
A cup of tea all ready
When Jesus comes to call.

# V   At the Drop of a Hat

One of my dearest friends, and certainly my first and most generous patron was Robert Morley. He was the first to put down money on his belief in my talent as a playwright.

'I think I will take a little option on this play of yours, dear,' he said, over supper at Caprice where he had introduced me to Terence Rattigan and Beatrice Lillie as 'Rosemary Anne Sisson, a brilliant playwright,' quite regardless of the fact that I could have furnished a bedsitter with my rejection slips. He accordingly wrote a cheque for £50 for a three-year option, and I wish that I had the cheque to frame and put on the wall of my study, but unfortunately I had to cash it because I needed the money.

It was many years before Robert and I actually got a play produced which we had written together, but meanwhile I joyously became part of his entourage and vicariously enjoyed his career, eating the Chinese meals which Ross Chatto somehow contrived to serve on stage and delighting in the outrageous excesses of his wit. I remember his humorous indignation when, appearing in a delightful musical called *Fanny*, he played to a vast, echoing, nearly empty Drury Lane while next door Flanders and Swann were packing their tiny theatre with a two-man show called *At The Drop Of A Hat*. It had a delicious spontaneity about it, as though those two, with their air of being mere talented amateurs, had just thought of something timely and funny and had written a song about it – a song which, oddly enough, turned out to be true and memorable.

This is the pleasure of writing 'occasional poetry', that it is spontaneous. You feel angry or sorrowful or amused, and instead of crying or laughing – or perhaps while crying or laughing – you write a poem. Some of these occasional pieces of mine were published, but for most of them it was enough just to write them in order to ease the soul or heart or temper.

Oh, how I love the human race!
I love its foolish, loving face.
When I am introduced to one,
I *always* say, 'What jolly fun!'

# Not on the Agenda (1)

I love the Old Etonians
Who passionately say
Society should be fairer –
They say it every day.

They care about the Working Man.
They never can forget him.
They use his name to serve their ends,
Although they've never met him.

Their sons to Comprehensive Schools
They diligently send.
That School it is in Camden
(The rather better end).

If private schools should be destroyed
To serve the Rights of Man,
At least it would get rid of
The Old Etonian.

# Not on the Agenda (2)

Do not be kind to the People.
It only gives them ideas.
Peers will be hung from lamp posts
And bureaucrats act like Peers.

# Boris Pasternak

What impulse, then? Merely a need to speak
Among so many silent? Minstrelsy,
Having a tale to tell, and hearers, never mind who?
Or that more lunative surge of emulation
Amidst the driven multitudes of men
Who live unknown and die too fast to cheer?

Or, more profound, more irresistible,
Out of the Russian winter of a life
Begun obscurely on one whirling sun
So many million years before this winter,
To raise another voice crying, 'I am!'
Others before have said it and been silenced.
Who now remembers those who silenced them?

# Ithaca

Ulysses came at last sailing
Home, oh home!
Saw the known headland and the
Rock-familiar foam.

Ulysses homeward, homeward
Came at last,
Stirred by grizzled recalling of
Things long past.

Ulysses came in the stillness,
Found no smile
Of welcoming wife or sons or friends on the
Barren isle.

Ulysses came at last sailing,
Tempest-tossed,
Cried, 'Every man, every man has his Ithaca –
'Lost, ah lost!'

# Lady Chatterly Replies

I'm suing the Gamekeeper for libel.
The things that he told Lawrence just aren't true.
I may have passed the time of day,
But I never slipped away
To his *horrid* little hut at half-past two.

My husband is so sorry it has happened.
As a Gamekeeper, the man is beyond praise.
But his manners are uncouth,
He's incapable of truth,
And I cannot understand a *word* he says!
     (Quite short words, too, some of them).

I'm suing the Gamekeeper for libel,
And those funny little paper books they sell.
In the *Tatler* or the *Queen*
One is willing to be seen,
But, my dear, to share a page with Penguins – *well!*

I'm suing the Gamekeeper for libel,
And the damages, let me tell you, won't be small.
I'm sure I cannot lose
When the Footman breaks the news
That it wasn't the Gamekeeper at all!

# Jamestown, 1619

*In 1619, a Dutch man-of-war brought the first Negro slaves*
*to America*

This bird most singular comes skimming
   Wave-wise, landwards, trimming
White sails swan-feather-flown,
   Bird singular, yet not alone.
     (Ships carry cargoes.)

The unembattled man-of-war
   Advancing on the pliant shore
Sounds no alarum to the years,
   Unheralded, no challenge hears.
     (Yet, ships carry cargoes.)

The Flying Dutchman comes at last
   To harbourage, its voyage past,
But in the oceans of the mind
   Eternally no rest can find.
     (Ships carry cargoes.)

The unexampled bargain made
   Of goods delivered, price unpaid,
From this time forward still must stand
   Upon the tallies of the land.
     (O ships carry cargoes!)

So from the sea this bird of prey
   Both brings and feeds upon decay,
And illustrates a tale untold –
   White sails, white sails, white sails, black hold!
     (Ships carry cargoes.)

# Normandy, Surrey

When William crossed the narrow sea,
What homesick conquering soldier came,
Ignored its former English name,
And called this village Normandy?

Or was it in his pride that he
Stamped down what it had been before,
And trod his native land once more,
Since where *he* trod was Normandy?

But, arrogant or homesick, he
Achieved a strange defeat at last.
This Norman, when the wars were past,
Found he had conquered – Normandy.

# Fulbright Seminar – Staying in University College, Oxford

In quadrangles cat-like stepping,
Female in the masculine night,
Delicately round the still, flagged paths,
Uneasily hermaphrodite.

Sleeping in flat, monastic bed,
In bath too long for woman's bone
Lying entombed, immarbled there,
Like wife in a Crusader's stone.

Seeing the alabaster limbs
Of Shelley cast upon the shore,
And in them all the other dead
Youths gone, youth gone for ever more.

Each stone close-mortared by the blood
Of young men gone, of young men died,
And she, this College, secretly
Not nourrisser but infanticide.

# Tristan da Cunha – No More

Perhaps they lied and cheated,
As other people do.
We were not there to see it.
Their weakness no one knew.

A bleak and rocky fortress,
Like honour in the heart,
They held their naked island.
They lived their life apart.

We did not ask to go there.
Enough to be assured
Simplicity and courage
Had somewhere still endured.

Unpeopled now they leave it,
In harsh volcanic showers.
Though they it is are homeless,
The loss, the loss is ours!

## Agammemnon, King of Greece

Agammemnon
Stepped about the thyme bush,
Wandered round the olive trees,
Saw his little town
Scented in the sunlight,
Baked in the dry folds
Of dull green grass
And brown Grecian land.

Agammemnon,
Little sandalled monarch,
Ruler of Mycenae,
Saw the lion arch
Baked like a coffee-mould,
Diminutively roaring,
Little sandalled monarch
Held the world in his hand.

Agammemnon
Bestrid like a Colossus
The great blue arch
Of Jupiter's sky,
King Agammemnon,
Poetic lord of tragedy,
Where warring armies surged
Up and down.

Agammemnon,
Victor of the Trojan Wars,
Famous in history till
The end of time,

Agammemnon,
Self-devoured monarch,
Lost forever
His small, thyme-scented town.

# For M.J.P. – Perfectionist

'Ah, but a man's reach should exceed his grasp,' said
   Browning,
'Or what's a Heaven for?' That theory stinks,
For he who follows it may arrive in Heaven
Much sooner than he thinks!

# Edenbridge

'Ruins,' said the Anglo-Saxon poet,
And spoke of men long dead, grip-fasted in the earth,
And we were there, wondering at a Tudor house,
The Priory, vestigially seen
In leper-windows in the dining-room,
The Roman road driving its flinty way
Through soft green fields, and oak and ash and thorn.

'Time,' said the Anglo-Saxon poet,
And felt the world tremble beneath his feet.
Still, as his poem the ruins did outlive,
We, on the lawn with dogs and children, saw
In this fast-flowing, Eden-encircled world,
Our fifteen-year-old friendship safely stand,
Stronger than stone, outlasting change and time.

# For the Lucasfilm Fourth of July
# Picnic

Once, a beloved child,
Half-venturesome, half-exiled,
    Sailed to a world unknown.

Through struggle and despair
And hardship everywhere,
    He made that land his own.

England, in folly frantic,
Across the broad Atlantic
    Cast off that child so dear.

But it was meant to be,
For children must be free,
    In spite of many a tear.

Happy are they at last
Who, when the pain is past
    And pride and anger end,

Can joyfully there meet
Where love and freedom greet –
    Nor child nor parent – friend!

# V.K.S. – 100th Birthday

A hundred years! That's a long time
To turn from history into rhyme!
But it's not history, it's your life,
Great-Gran and Gran, Mother and Wife,
And we here try to understand
That life of which we're all a strand –
Nieces and nephews, great and small –
But please remember, best of all
We celebrate in love, not duty,
One who was and still is a beauty.
Charlie, unknown to many here,
Loved to the end his Babs so dear,
And beauty is not just of face –
Charming, but even more of grace.
For grace a hundred years may live.
Dear Mom, it has! Our love we give.

# VI   That Old Familiar – Death

After my parents were back in London, living in that
tall, elegant, inconvenient Queen Anne house in Chelsea, I would come home on leave from the Observer
Corps, painfully aware, as they were not, of the extent
to which the flying bombs were falling in clusters all
around us. One night, I remember, I got up and, sick
with terror, crept into my sister's bed, feeling for the
first time the full anguish of that Elizabethan poem
written during the plague: '*Timor mortis conturbat me.*'
The bombs came close but missed us, and I have never
been afraid of death again.

When you are young, you think that the world can
be made perfect, and you know exactly how it should
be done. But as you grow older, you realise that people
are always going to be stupid and greedy and incompet-
ent, that the good aren't all good and that the wicked
aren't all bad, and that they're all going to make a mess
of it as usual. So at last the time comes when you say,
'Well, thank goodness, *I* won't be here to see it!' The
poem about lemmings came to me when I was standing
at a bus stop in New King's Road, waiting as usual for
a 22 bus. I ransacked my handbag in vain for a piece of
paper, but I found an old bus ticket in my pocket and
wrote it on that, rather small.

But it's one thing to accept death for yourself, and
quite another to acquiesce in the death of others. Some-
times I think that death is like a knife which cuts a
little more and a little more – and then at last to the
quick! And the worst part of the death of those we love
is the way they seem to vanish into a kind of limbo, so
that suddenly we can hardly even remember what they
look like. I believe that it is God's way of gently separat-

ing the living from the dead, and that if we truly love them, they return at last and never leave us again.

After Bishop's death, the garden of Church Field, despite our best, feeble endeavours, declined into a wilderness, and my parents sold it and with the proceeds bought a tall, ugly Victorian house in Fulham. 'Let's go where the crocuses grow,' we had said, when the Chelsea rent began to soar, and so it was that we found ourselves in Parson's Green, that friendliest of all London villages. Fulham, like Lyminster, has become yuppified, and there sure as hell ain't no sticklebacks or newts on Eel Brook Common, but this is now my home and I know that this is the place where I want to live and die.

After thirty years, my part of the house is crammed beyond overflowing with scripts and books and all the absurd but treasured photographs and memorabilia of a lifetime spent in the theatre and television and adjacent arts. Now and then I remember that narrow bed under thatch with the bombers thrumming overhead and the blue cardboard suitcase packed with Edward Bear and the blue suit with the Juliet cap and the manuscript of the (still unpublished!) novel. And, as Death's Winged Chariot thunders close, I think, well, all I really want to take with me is this book of poems.

# Quia Impossibile

Who believes that he will die?
Not I!

See the uncomplaining sun
Finish what he has begun,
Returning on the sequent day
As he had never been away.
See the birds each fragrant spring
Speed upon instinctive wing
To the place where they would be,
Fragments of eternity.

See the buds, through winter's pall,
Quicken as the brown leaves fall.
Who believes that he shall die?
Not I!

But, waking in the dead of night,
It's hard to keep the birds in sight.
When the rain soaks in the sod,
Harder still to trust in God.

# Beau, 1939–1948

Our darling Beau we bury here
In this small corner set apart.
This space is not so large, my dear,
As that you still hold in my heart.

Silenced is now the hideous roar
Of gunfire that distracted you.
You will not fear it any more.
But, ah, your voice is silenced, too.

Indomitable, faithful, gay,
Making each dwelling-place a home,
Could *those* nine years seem like a day?
And what, then, of the years to come?

The poet's friends his death will mourn.
The lover shall his love be-cry.
But what faint tears will serve my turn?
For Lear without his Fool am I.

# Go Cheerful

When my time has come to die,
I hope that there may be
To bid farewell to me
A brilliant, cloudlessly-blue sky.

I hope the lilac is in bloom,
And daffodils may dance,
And tulips bend and glance,
And sunlight stream into the room.

Don't draw the curtains, don't pull down the blind,
And don't wear sombre dress.
Don't think of ugliness,
If to my memory you would be kind.

Please ask the Minister to speak of me
As one who trod
Life's path with God.
Oh, let his words ring out in glorious certainty!

Plant flowers there among the grass
Whose cheerful bloom
And sweet perfume
May please the churchgoers who pass.

Oh, don't let dying make my memory false!
Put in my epitaph
How much I loved to laugh,
And that I loved to dance to an old-fashioned waltz.

# Mr Pullen Dying

He is dying. He is dying.
No good to say now, 'The fine weather will help him.'
'It's the fog. It's the rain. The doctors must do
    something.'
But what can one say, now that he's dying?
What is the formula now for consolation?

All that great strength and the rough, healthy voice
Dwindled to a death-mask on a pale pillow,
A tender, small, child-sleeping figure in the wide bed,
The cancered chest rising and falling, soon to be still.
Where will she sleep now, after he's gone?

Not to know, not to know where he has gone,
Only that the marriage has ended, as though he,
Weary of coughing, pain and weakness,
Silently left, and was gone forever,
Leaving her for the first time in all their marriage alone.

And yet, it wasn't quite like that. He said to her,
'I'm going to die.' After all the months
Of lies and evasions, they met there together
A few weeks ago, as so often before
On saving for the holidays or the boy's school blazer.

And for all his shouting at the children, his rough teasing,
His last thought was not to spoil the grandchildren's
    holiday,
Not to interrupt his daughter's week at Worthing.
That was the last promise he insisted she should make –
The promise which, heartbroken, she still couldn't break.

To have lived so close, each to each other,
In sickness and health unsentimentally committed,
Speaking so harshly, but in the last cruel months
Softened like lovers, arm in racked arm,
Did this lead only to the silent ride to Putney and the
    name on the crematorium wall and then nothing?

Isn't there some glory, not like the pearly gates,
Not like the Resurrection in flowing white robes,
Some honest, believable, linoleum-floored heaven,
Framed for a man like this, who lived and died with such
    honour,
Fit for this true-loving pair who lived in Fulham?

# The Death of Irwin Edman

To see in small print in an English paper
A transatlantic end,
Casually, at the breakfast table,
The death of an American friend.
To have written a letter to the dead,
And not to remember what you said.

Then the blessed shock of the resurrection,
That blind scrawl leaping across the room,
And the envelope coming readily open,
Like a stone rolled away from the mouth of a tomb.
'So pleased with your letter.' How like him to sever
Acquaintance so gracefully – ending, 'Yours ever!'

# What's Wrong with Lemmings?

What's wrong with lemmings? Lemmings know
This is the end, and on they go.
Though wiser lemmings say, 'Hold back!'
And greedy lemmings have a snack,
More idealistically inclined
Lemmings rush on, unheeding, blind,
Engrossing in their lemming heart
The world of which they once felt part,
Rejecting with their lemming feet
An over-populated cheat.
What's wrong with lemmings? Lemmings know
Exactly when it's time to go.

# Gently into the Night

Gently into the night,
Gently, gently into the night,
Once so dreaded, now a friend,
The calm, inevitable end,
Welcomed at last without a fight.

Only for me the grief.
Only for me the nightmare grief,
The dead face on the tomb,
The silent, death-filled room,
The haunted disbelief.

Gently, Poppa, at last,
Gently, gently returned at last.
No more the study set apart,
No more the limbo of the heart.
All that is safely past,
And night is gone at last.


# Lines on a Dying Father

Seeing no ending but the one we dread,
Seeing no exit but the one marked 'dead'

# Uninvited Death

Comes uninvited death once, only once
And takes him unawares,
Pulls the still latch and softly steals him sleeping,
Or topples him down the neglected stairs.

# Death of a Friend

Ashes to ashes, dust to dust.
She died at last, as die she must.
But, oh the worst – the very worst! –
It was her spirit that died first.

# Timor Mortis Conturbat Me

By guess and by God,
Barefoot or go shod,
We travel this earth
In sorrow and mirth,
In storm and in rain,
Then sunshine again,
In anguish and wrath
Still seeking the path
Of contentment and peace
Freehold bought, not just lease,
But no pain without joy,
Intermixed, an alloy,
So, defeated, we strive,
Knowing just we're alive,
Till at last we lose breath.
Then there's taxes and death.

# In Memoriam Ted Willis

'Have you asked Ted?' we used to say
When problems came to light.
He never failed to answer –
And mostly he was right.

I told him of a problem
Which one day might arise
In my own life – ridiculous!
He looked me in the eyes.

He didn't joke or laugh it off.
'Ring any time,' he said.
How many others heard those words?
And now that he is dead

We all will have to honour him
By trying to fill the space
So warm and generous which he left –
That very special grace.

I am a Christian. Ted was not.
The gift he left behind
I wish we could achieve so well –
His love for all mankind.

# Familiar Things

I like familiar things,
The hand upon the switch,
The foot upon the step,
The known bird that sings.

A squashed chip on the pavement?
I know the reason why –
The fish and chip shop in the Lane nearby,

Intimate interlocking
Of circumstance and thought,
Things running as they ought.

So, with a little jar,
It comes about at last
That in a while death
Becomes familiar.

# Lyminster Churchyard

I would rise from my grave, I said, for just that smell
Of river and marsh,
I would rise from my grave, yes, rise from my coffin's cell.

Though my feet were only bone, I would walk as so often
    before
Sightless down the lane,
Over the ruts and flints, though my feet were only bone –
    skeleton light, skeleton sure.

But, my gentle friends, don't fear that I will rise and
    walk.
Only bury me here
With the smell of the river and marsh, and I will lie in my
    grave, one with the clay and the chalk.